HOW TO RUN
A THRIFTY KITCHEN

Advice from the Ancestors,
edited and updated for
MODERN LIVING

A
RETROMETRO
TECHNOBOOK

Published by CL Leavey & Co,
A3 The Green Business Centre
Stanford Bridge, Worcestershire WR6 6SA

Retro Metro Technobooks No.2
ISBN 978-0-9570768-1-5

British Library Cataloguing in Publication Data. A catalogue
record for this book is available from the British Library.

Printed in Great Britain by
Orphans Press, Leominster

Set throughout in Gill Sans,
first used on a shopfront by Eric Gill in 1926

Cover illustration taken from a
lead printer's block, C.1925

Please drop in to download digital editions,
pick up factsheets, buy random stuff
and join our mailing list, at:

www.RETROMETRO.co

CONTENTS

HOW TO RUN
A THRIFTY KITCHEN

FOREWORD

"When a man finds himself faced with a cut in income of at least 10%, an increase in income tax equal to about 5% of his income, and the pound miserably shrunk to seven-tenths of its original size, he does not merely discuss economy as an abstract proposition or an ideal, he acts.

"Man can economise in diet, but here, as everywhere else, there is a true and a false economy. Cutting down what one spends upon food is not necessarily economy. Getting the same food value at less cost is, and it is the purpose of this book to show an easy way of doing so."

VH Mottram, "Sound Catering for Hard Times", 1932

As a child, during the early Seventies, I knew what it was to play board games by the light of a single paraffin lamp, and to wear my (male) cousins' clothes. But I didn't know what it was to go hungry. My mother was born during the depression, and was four at the start of World War 2. She didn't go hungry either. Both those periods of history were times when money, and the stuff you might buy with it, were in short supply – and the thrifty expertise of previous generations was dusted off and put to excellent use.

And so we find ourselves in another one of those hard-to-handle eras, and I find myself a mother in troubled times like my mother and my grandmother before me. But I've had to adjust not at all, because not only did they train me well; I also have my collection of household books yelling hot tips at me on all sides. Added to which, I've been practicing the more extreme forms of penny-pinching since long before

That Crisis laid waste to a world in which the popular image of debt had become dangerously detoxified. In 2005, my business was stolen away from under me, and I suddenly found myself with a monthly income of £535 and a monthly mortgage payment of £545. I sold a few things, grew a few things, gutted and skinned a fair amount of roadkill, performed a few financial back-flips, and for several years both my collection of old household books – and my childhood training – were stretched right up to breaking point. But in the event, nothing broke. I struggled through, I won that horrible private war – and I also learnt some extra stuff first-hand.

I learnt that every penny shaved off a bill will join forces with other pennies shaved off other bills to make a veritable army. Many of the tricks you'll find here, like saving the plastic outers from junk mail, and cadging the odd un-green plastic carrier bag, might sound pathetic when a roll of sandwich bags or bin liners is only three or four pounds. But when you think that's three or four pounds you could be spending on milk or eggs or flour, and when you think how much fresh, delicious bread and soup, and pancakes and cakes, and puddings and sandwiches you could be producing with that milk and flour, and those eggs, suddenly you come to love those salvaged plastic bags you're smoothing flat and folding like a tragic Orphan Annie, and to realise the true – enormous – value of those very few, very hard-won pounds.

Once upon a time, whether you had charge of a household of servants, or toiled in the dinge of your own tiny scullery, you had a deep technical understanding of the food you consumed, and you made maximum use of every scrap – of anything – that passed through your hands. With more dark times ahead, and with the era of artificially 'cheap' food and fuel now drawing to a close, it's time for us all to rediscover and reclaim the power to feed ourselves.

And to do so deliciously.

Claire Leavey
October 2012

———————◆———————

5

1: PLAN, SHOP, STORE

The one essential skill you'll need in running a thrifty kitchen is planning. And to plan effectively, you need to think about storage — and buying.

Better Storage

Modern fitted kitchen cupboards are a nightmare for efficiency, since they are so deep that many purchases get swallowed up in their depths, only to resurface when they're so out of date that they have to be scraped off the cupboard floor. Fitted cupboards get musty, too. Even early kitchenettes, forerunners of the fitted kitchen, had ventilation.

Better to keep ingredients arranged on a large rank of shallow shelves, so that the air can move round them, and you can see at a glance what you have, and what needs to be replenished. Making up a list is so easy if everything is laid out clearly in front of you. And how about this for a dream scenario: you're standing in the pantry, maybe with a cup of tea at hand, checking stock levels off against an electronic spreadsheet on your iPad, and inputting any shortages straight into your basket on the grocer's website. Heaven!

Open shelves will also save lots of wasted rummaging time when you need to quickly knock something up. Custom-fitting the shelves is easy, and if you have a cupboard under the stairs, or an old brick larder or similar, preferably still with its air-brick or small gauze-covered window intact, you will be very well served if you resurrect this by fitting it out with some nicely measured slats. In Chapter 7 you'll find plans for the brackets, and instructions for constructing the whole shelving system. Design the shelves to accommodate big glass jars, decanting packets straight into them, and you'll have an elegant and functional feature wall — and an instant view of what you have, too.

Larder Ideals

If possible, the larder should face north, but if this can't be managed, the window should be shaded and covered with wire gauze to keep out flies. The larder must be perfectly dry, and well ventilated. If the walls are not tiled, they should be white-washed, and the counter should be white-tiled, made of marble, slate, or stone, or covered in aluminium sheet. Keep it all spotlessly clean.

A large store-cupboard is necessary in every house, and it should be perfectly dry and well ventilated. All soaps and other cleaning materials should be kept apart from the foodstuffs. And jams, sauces, and pickles should be stored in the driest possible corner as they will ferment with warmth or damp.

The Freezer

The freezer is probably the single most useful thing you can add to a modern thrifty kitchen's armoury. Here you can store leftovers like stale bread, breadcrumbs or cooked veg while they accumulate, keep fresh-frozen herbs, bulk-bought bargains, home-made stock and catfood; and even batch-cooked ready meals and baked treats, making it a matter of elegant luxury to whip out an urgent tea loaf, a lasagne, a pie, or a sprinkle of coriander for that delicious tagine. Get the biggest freezer you can accommodate, for you will surely fill it – and get the best quality, most energy-efficient you can afford. Not only will this save on running costs now, it'll also extend its useful life. Cheap freezers tend to die young, and also get sick and doddery long before that, so hoovering up a shocking amount of electricity.

A giant freezer will pay for itself many times over. For example, a big bag of frozen fish or chicken is considerably cheaper than the fresh alternative. Take a look next time you're in a supermarket. For a real thrill, compare the price of fresh versus frozen sausages. Go for high-value items when buying for the freezer, by the way; why fill it with cheap stuff like oven chips and garlic bread when you can store flour and potatoes in the pantry at a running cost of zero?

Fresh Food in the Pantry

All sorts of fresh foods will store very well in a cool pantry. Fresh fruit and veg should stay good for up to a week, but once cut they should be moved to the refrigerator. Even then, if you remove whole leaves from cabbages as you need them, the rest of the head will keep perfectly well until it's all gone! A loosely tied plastic bag is always very useful for keeping fresh produce from losing moisture. Baskets will make sure nothing falls from the shelves, and potatoes should be stored underneath the shelving, in their paper sack, to prevent them from going green. Salads and herbs will stay fresh standing in water.

Storing for the Well Run Kitchen

The goods you buy to supply a properly run kitchen will be raw ingredients, versatile in their possible uses, and ideally suited to long-term storage. In place of that spongy, unsatisfactory bag loaf (life: 1 week) you'll have a 3kg bag of strong plain flour (life: 1 year, and also usable for making pizza, pitta, baps, and even crumpets or scotch pancakes), and you'll add to it a little dried yeast, some salt, and a little oil from a gallon bottle, which were all conveniently waiting on the shelf. In place of that chilled pasta sauce in the expensive disposable plastic pot (so binning about 30p), you'll have a carton of passata (life: 2½ years), an onion, some garlic, maybe some shavings off the parma ham you keep hanging overhead (life: 1 year), a sprinkle of capers or nasturtium seeds from a little jar, and a slug of oil from the gaily-painted gallon can you'll use next year to grow a tomato plant. Sugar will arrive in 5kg sacks, and will disappear rapidly as you use it for making glorious jams, chutneys, sauces, puddings and cakes.

Buying Clever

By buying dried or canned goods in multipacks or in bigger containers (ie, sacks of rice, onions or potatoes; gallon cans of oil), you will find you save a lot of money. If you organise your storage logically, with products grouped as you'd find them in a supermarket, they can still be quickly snatched off the shelf as needed, and huge unmanageable packs can be decanted into containers of a handier size, these then topped up as necessary. Most packaged products (like sugar, pasta, pulses, tomato, fruit juice, soup, coconut milk, custard, tinned goods, rice and so on) will have a shelf life of at least a year, as will cooking oils, so there is absolutely no point in buying these sorts of things little and often. Larger volumes are cheaper to process, pack and handle, and this saving is always factored into the price at the till. Especially if you go to a sensibly practical shop, like an Indian supermarket, one of the no-frills supermarkets, or a cash-and-carry.

To plan bulk shopping effectively, first think through an average week, and the kinds of things you might like to eat on each day. Now work out how frequently you might repeat that meal, to find the total volume of all the ingredients needed for that dish during, say, a month. Do this for several meals, and there you have a practical and efficient list, with volume estimates, for your first bulk shop. Shopping in bulk once a month or so is the norm in most country homes, and there's no reason why urban kitchens shouldn't be run in the same, super-efficient way. Planned bulk buying also means you'll save a lot of fuel, (or delivery charges), and certainly time.

Luxuries

Luxuries like chocolate cake, fresh pasta and oven chips don't need to be abandoned in the interests of thrift. In fact, making your own pasta is cheap – and far more nutritious than subsisting on the dried kind. And of course if you can't buy a machine, tone your upper arms for free by using a rolling pin! Enough **Fresh Pasta for Two** people is yours for the price of 4oz (100g) 00 flour and one egg. Both are on the pantry shelf. **Oven chips?** You have a sack of potatoes on the pantry floor. Boil thick-cut potatoes (Maris Piper are the best variety) for five to eight minutes, at the same time heating a roasting tin with around 50ml sunflower oil to 200°C. Drain the potatoes well and put into the hot oil (it will spit), turning a few times to coat, then place in the oven for twenty minutes, turning once or twice to brown evenly. They didn't take up any precious freezer space, and and they will taste so much better than the ones that came in a bag. And if you ever fancy a chocolate cake at short notice, just make sure you have a big bar of good cooking chocolate and a tub of cocoa powder on the shelf.

A Word on Shelf Life and Stock Management

It maybe helps you to understand how this new way of shopping is best managed, if you think that the word 'store', as applied to shops, comes from the days when communities would manage a communal storeroom, into which produce was placed by local producers, and goods were then drawn off by individual households, often on a barter system. The 'professional' grocery practices of stock rotation, grouping of goods for easy selection, and 'facing up' of labels, have always been equally good practice in private stores, whether we're thinking of an under-stairs larder, or a purpose-built facility at the centre of a feudal village. 'Rotating' stock means moving the older items to the front of the shelf and replenishing with new stock at at the back, by the way, so ensuring that things never languish forgotten, quietly expiring.

Avoid bulk-buying anything ready-ground, since these products lose flavour and goodness very much faster than the unprocessed versions. I wouldn't go so far as to buy wheat and make my own flour, but I would certainly never buy coffee or spices ready-ground. Any coffee grinder (brushed clean first) will quickly tackle spices, and even small volumes of seed or grain to add interest to loaves.

To quote Alfred H Miles, writing in *'Everybody's Household Guide'* (1904), "The store room is the arsenal of the household".

And yes, when wheat prices are soaring, a big sack of flour can be a powerful weapon.

2: FUEL EFFICIENCY

It's not just in how you buy and use your foodstuffs that you run a thrifty kitchen. As fuel prices continue to climb skywards, how you actually do the cooking will make a *massive* difference to your household bills too. Here we'll start from the ground up, looking at the best sort of fuel and cooker, and then we'll look at some excellent tricks and gadgets you can use to get the maximum bang for every buck you have to spend on fuel. First we'll think about the sort of fuel you want (or have) to use.

Free Fire

Cooking with wood or solid fuel is in fact my preference, and it's fantastically quick and convenient – if, that is, you have the energy for carting the fuel about, the extra time to devote to raising and controlling the fire, and the knowledge needed to use this very versatile type of stove to best advantage. Even without a special cooker, or even much study, if you have an open fire or a woodburner, investing in a little lidded cast iron Dutch oven (or aluminium Dutch pot) to sit in the embers means that you can cook stews, roast meat, and bake potatoes – or even bread – on your existing sitting-room fire, without spending a single extra penny on fuel! And the flavour of food cooked in this way just can't be beaten. Just remember that a Dutch oven sitting in the strongly glowing embers of a burnt-down log fire gives such an instant and powerful heat that you'll have to watch whatever you're cooking very carefully indeed to make sure it doesn't burn. Stews can boil dry in an instant, and jacket potatoes will need occasional shaking about to prevent them charring on one side!

Gas

Gas, unless it's bottled LPG for off-grid homes, is, per therm, definitely the cheaper of the two most common cooking fuel options. And for anyone who spends much time away from the home, gas is the perfect fuel, since it gives instant, controllable heat, and doesn't need to be watched and gauged in the same way as a natural fire. And you can get away with using quite a cheap hob, too, since its quality of manufacture and design will have little to do with how economically you run it. Just be sure to always have the flame neatly tucked under the base of the pan, and fuel waste will be kept to a minimum. For the oven, some people do prefer electricity, mainly because cheap gas ovens can give localised heat and so can cook unevenly. Here you can just remember to turn things from time to time – or of course consider spending a bit extra to get a really well thought-out burner design.

Electricity

If you're stuck with only electricity, however, all is not lost. For it's in cooking electrically that you stand to make the biggest savings on your current bills, just by applying a little ingenuity to how you use the fuel, and maybe by changing your equipment to something that also improves your cooking experience beyond measure…

A conventional ring or ceramic electrical hob takes a long time to heat up and cool down, so you have to constantly think ahead in order to avoid burning things, or to make sure they're ready in time to go with something else. The cheaper or older the cooker, the less controllable and the slower to heat and cool (so wasteful of fuel) it will be. The fuel wasted in the slow heat-up can't really be helped – though you should always make sure you've put the pan on the ring before turning it on, since this will at least help it to get to temperature more quickly. Also ensure that the pan is matched neatly to the size of the ring, otherwise you'll be paying extra to heat the air around a too-small pan. You can though save quite a bit of fuel by turning the ring down or even off before the cooking is actually finished. The exact timing will depend on your knowledge of your own cooker, and how long it takes to cool down – but I used to regularly save ten to twenty minutes' worth of full-pelt electricity per meal just by doing this. The bigger the pan and the harder it's boiling when you turn off the ring, the longer you'll get of this 'free' cooking time. Solid electric hobs will stay hot for longer than the coiled rings, by the way.

To get your electricity bills down to their absolute minimum, some up-front investment is, sadly, required. An induction hob (not to be confused with the cheap, inefficient ceramic hobs) works by means of magnetism to heat iron, steel and enamel pans ferociously quickly, and using a tiny amount of fuel. You can also do away with the ugly clutter of a microwave if you have an induction hob; the speed and fuel efficiency are roughly comparable, and the food comes out properly cooked and appealing – for a change! Induction hobs are about twice the price of the 'best' conventional type; you'll also have to double-check that your pans will work on them, since not all do. To get the full fuel-saving benefit of an induction hob, it's really little use buying one of those adaptor plates that allows you to use your old non-ferrous pans. Even then, the short-term pain of converting to induction will fade into memory the first time you experience the instant boil, and the shrinking electricity bill...

Another upfront expense that will minimise your future electricity consumption is to change an old-fashioned wired-in oven for a super-efficient 13-amp one. I still find it hard to believe that I swapped a vibrating, buzzing, power-guzzling, slow-to-heat oven whose shielded cable was stiff with solid copper cores for one with a flimsy, slender lead that plugs into a normal socket and heats to 230°C in a couple of minutes. Really high-quality, efficient electrical equipment like this is also the perfect back-up for an Aga or a wood stove, particularly in Summer when you don't want to run these monsters all the time.

The Pressure Cooker

Every kitchen should have a pressure cooker. Not only does it save masses of fuel, but it also makes running the kitchen an awful lot easier and more convenient. It can be used for sterilising preserves, hugely accelerates the cooking of stock, stews, rice, pulses, beetroot, potatoes etc, and even provides the necessary capacity for making quite large volumes of chutney or jam. Whole books have been written on the subject, so I shall simply point you towards them. Buy one. Embrace its hissing drama. Don't be scared of it, for if you follow the manufacturer's guidelines for use, nothing will go wrong. And if you have an induction hob, make sure you buy a pressure cooker made of suitably high-ferrous stainless steel, or get an adaptor plate, so you can actually use it!

Pan Savvy

Cheap pans waste fuel. That's all there is to it. And they're more inclined to heat unevenly, and to burn, which then makes the pan more likely to burn again in the same place in future. I would seriously prefer to struggle through life with a single really good pan than an entire *batterie de cuisine* of cheap pans bought in a 'super value' set from a high street shop. The more expensive pans are heavier, because they're made using more of their expensive conductive materials; they have expensive hidden expertise in their bases which makes heat more evenly distributed, more readily absorbed, and retained in the pan for longer; and there's expertise hidden in their lids, too, which means maximum convection of the heat inside. So they make better food and use less fuel. They'll also last you a lifetime, and could potentially save you from one or two dangerous accidents, too, as the handles usually come loose and drop off the cheapest ones.

Store pans with their lids off and they won't become musty smelling. Never use washing soda on an aluminium pan because it will dissolve it. Burnt pans need not always be thrown out; the gentlest solution is to fill them with salt and water and leave overnight. The next day bring slowly to boiling point, then wash. The burnt material should come off easily. Scrubbing with whiting mixed to a paste with water will remove burnt-on material from aluminium pans. Aluminium is cleaned beautifully using horsetail, a plant found in most wet or damp places in England. Make a brush by tightly tying together several three-inch pieces of the stem in two places, about half an inch apart, leaving two brush-like ends. Boil an onion in a burnt saucepan and the burnt material will rise to the top of the water. New enamel saucepans will last much longer if you first prepare them for use by placing in a pan of cold water, bringing slowly to the boil, and then allowing them to cool in the water. This could also be done in the oven if the pan has a heatproof handle. Burnt enamel saucepans can be cleaned by boiling up washing soda and water, then allowing to simmer for a little while. A squirt of washing-up liquid in a little water, simmered for ten minutes or so, will often serve just as well. Prevent milk from boiling over by putting a pie funnel in the pan. The boiling milk will run up and through this, so preventing any wasteful eruptions.

Keep pans clean and in good condition to keep them working at their most efficient. Pans furred up with hard water deposits, or with caked-on black stuff on the exterior, use more fuel to heat, and they will heat unevenly. Throw out a cheap pan if it gets burnt, and relish the opportunity to replace it with a more expensive one, which won't get so easily scorched and spoilt, and will give you a perfectly inappropriate thrill of pleasure every time you use it.

The Steamer

You can get away with using a single ring to cook every vegetable needed for a meal, simply by use of a stacking steamer. The cheap bamboo Chinese ones are ideal inside a large saucepan if you are only feeding one or two people; but for a family of four or more, a stacking stainless steel arrangement on top of the pan is a dream. Boil potatoes in the bottom, put carrots, sprouts etc in the next layer up (where the the steam is hottest), moving higher still to tender things in need of gentler treatment, like asparagus, broccoli and cauliflower.

Some Fuel-Saving Tricks PLAN

When you're roasting a joint, bulk-roast a big tin of vegetables alongside to make maximum use of the oven. The surplus of these following the meal can then be kept in the fridge, to serve in stews, fried rice, pasta sauce, soups and so on during the coming week.

Similarly, fill the oven whenever baking (it all cooks happily at 180°C), and freeze the extra. Baked goods thaw quickly, and can be used as normal as soon as they're up to room temperature. Bread rolls and baguettes can be part-baked (five minutes at a pre-heated 180°C) and frozen, then the frozen items thrown straight into the oven, for a quick, fresh-baked treat. Boil the kettle to fill the pan for cooking pasta. This uses much less fuel than heating a panful of water from cold. Dried noodles can be cooked inside a wide-necked Thermos, if they're covered with boiling water and sealed up for just three or four minutes or so. Apple sauce, pasta sauce, cooked rice and pulses will all save huge amounts of fuel if you make a big batch and then freeze it in useful portions. Grill a double quantity of sausages, and then have a super-quick toad-in-the-hole in a few days' time. Do the same with mashed potatoes, and enjoy a shepherd's pie or fishcakes later in the week. You'll save time, as well as fuel, if complex meals like lasagne, curries, fancy stews, pies and so on are made in multiples and then frozen for use as ready meals. Freeze lasagnes once assembled but before baking; and before freezing pies, bake them for five to ten minutes at a pre-heated 180°C to set the outer surface of the pastry, and then bake from frozen for best results.

The Thermal Cooker

Here is where we get into the good stuff. A thermal cooker (or haybox) is something you may be unfamiliar with – but by the time you reach the end of this little book I'm pretty sure you will have been prompted to either buy or build one. It's ideal for use in making stock and casseroles, in cooking up pulses and rice, in rendering down fruit and vegetables in the first stage of jam, syrup, sauce and chutney making, in making steamed puddings, and really, for just about any job which demands slowish cooking over the course of several hours. You can even cook a super tender roast while saving fuel, by slow cooking in the haybox and then removing the meat to the oven to brown and crisp the outer surface. Essentially, it's a big stockpot type pan with an insulated outer. You boil up the pan on the hob, then put it inside the container, closely covered, to continue cooking in its own retained heat for several hours. Once the contents of the pan are boiling and enclosed, no further fuel is consumed. You're also spared constant cooking smells, so a haybox is great for anyone living in a studio or other cramped situation. You don't need to watch the pot once it's gone into the cooker, and food doesn't have the opportunity to dry onto the pan, so making the washing-up a great deal easier. Suddenly you'll find you can cook while you're out and about, and you'll have an embarrassment of spare time. And with fuel savings estimated at something like 90%, your energy supplier will probably also notice that you've got one pretty soon.

There are smart, hygienic readymade thermal cookers available, but you do have to hunt them down. Brands include 'Mr D's Thermal Cookers', the 'Empress' Magic Cooker, and the Thermos Shuttle Chef, which is the type I've used regularly for something like fifteen years. But making one is, if you have just a little skill and patience (plus a pan of a suitable shape and size), pretty straightforward, and will reduce the upfront investment needed from upwards of £50 for a readymade version, to just a few pounds for one made from bits of this and that.

Making a Haybox

The pan for a haybox should have straight sides, and ideally should be roughly square in proportions. The size should really be no less than four pints (two litres) since anything smaller won't cook so efficiently. It should have a close-fitting lid, and preferably top-mounted loop handle(s), making it easier to fit the insulation around it. You'll also need an outer box with a lid which is or can be hinged and secured. Match the box to the size of the pan you plan to use inside it, allowing a good few inches on all sides to accommodate the insulation. This can be hay, straw, paper, wool, mineral wool, or even sawdust. Wool is probably the best insulating material, and doesn't weigh too much, making it ideal for a haybox that has to be moved around. Wool insulation sheets are available from eco-building stores, and they're easy to tear up to work with, too. For a loose dry insulation, first line the interior of any wooden box with thick paper. A more permanent and elaborate (though heavier) insulation can be made up using vermiculite or perlite loose fill (available from woodburning stove specialists), mixed with cement in a ratio of four parts vermiculite to one part cement, plus just enough water to get the mixture to hold together. For using this mix, first cover the pan with plastic sheet or greaseproof paper to prevent the wet insulation from sticking to it, and make sure you can get good purchase on the handles to pull it out again! Pack the wet mix down firmly with a block of wood. Pack a firm layer of insulating material no less than three or four inches (10cm) deep in the base of the box. The pan should now sit about 3 to 5 inches below the lid when closed. With the pan in the centre of the box, pack round it tightly with insulation up to the level of the rim. Now carefully slip the pan out of the insulation and it should leave a neat hole. Lining the box with cloth, or with cardboard and paper, will help to keep the insulation in place, and will protect it from any spills. Finally, a cushion of insulation should be made to fit over the top of the pan. This can be made of any old fabric that comes to hand, and it should be stuffed loosely so that it can fit around the contours of the pan lid, and so that it completely fills the top of the box when the outer lid is closed. Avoiding air gaps between pan and insulation is critical to the success of your design.

Materials needed for making a haybox: an outer box, strong hinges (plus screws), a latch (plus screws), insulation material, a suitable pan (of 4 pints/2 litres or more), paper or fabric for interior lining, fabric for the top cushion, strong paper for lining out a wooden box.

Using a Thermal Cooker

Try to always use the thermal cooker as full as possible, since it will hold its heat better and cook faster. Keep the insulating box as near to the cooker as possible, since speed in transferring the pan from hob to box is essential. Heat the pan until its contents are thoroughly heated through and bubbling fiercely, then whip into the box and close tightly as quickly as you can. Keep the lid tightly closed throughout the cooking period. If the lid should be opened before the food is done, return it to the hob and reheat it to boiling point before shutting it down once more. Thermal cooking times will inevitably be longer than for dishes cooked entirely on the hob, and the larger the pieces of food, the longer they will need to cook before they are thoroughly heated through. Experimentation with time is very much the order of the day – but the worst that can happen is that things need to be reboiled and returned to the box to cook for a little longer, so the process of learning is well worth the effort. The Thermos Shuttle Chef cooks brown rice in around 45 minutes, and steamed puddings (the covered basin sitting on a trivet inside the cooker pan, half-filled with water) take approximately half as long again as they otherwise would (ie, a two-pint basin takes about three hours rather than two).

Two Recipes for a Home-made Thermal Cooker

Both of these recipes are perfect for working parents, since if you make them in the morning, they're ready just when you're most exhausted. The heat starts to go out of the cooker after a few hours, so eventually it just keeps the food ready to serve whenever needed.

Split Pea Soup. 1 pint (500ml) dried split peas, 4 pints (2 litres) cold water, 1 large soup bone, 2¾ teaspoons salt, ¼ teaspoon pepper. Soak the peas overnight and drain them. Wash the bone, boil it for ten minutes in the water and skim it, add the peas and seasoning, bring to the boil, and put into the cooker for four hours or more. Take out the bone and serve the soup, liquidised or in its natural state as you prefer. The peas should be cooked until they fall to pieces easily when well beaten. If desired, the meat may be taken from the bone, cut into small pieces, and served in the soup.

Braised Chicken. Roast a young, tender, cleaned chicken in a hot oven until it is brown. Put it into the preheated cooker pan with water about one inch deep in the bottom. Cover it quickly, bring to the boil, and put into the cooker for about two and a half hours or more. When the bird is ready to serve, make a proper gravy in the roasting tin, using the liquor from the cooker pan. You can also, if you have them, add the giblets when the chicken is put into the water, then chop them up and add them to the gravy too. Older, tougher birds can be cooked half-covered in water for ten to twelve hours, then finished in the oven, basted occasionally with fat skimmed from surface of the cooking water.

3: CHEAP TREATS

Living on healthy, low-budget food doesn't have to be a penance. Think your way around what you can make by being just a little clever with basic ingredients, and you'll find that life just gets more delicious the less you spend on it. These super-cheap, super-quick recipes are all indulgent and very tasty.

Quick, Easy and Delicious Savings

Fancy Porridge. Make nourishing and sustaining porridge for two using 2oz plain rolled oats to a pint (500ml) whole milk. Boil up, then simmer gently, stirring constantly to prevent sticking. If you've a good ferocious hob it can be ready in five minutes – though the longer the oats can soak up the milk, the nicer it becomes; so you might like to make the basic porridge at bed-time, then in the morning just quickly re-heat it, splosh in a bit more milk to make it really sloppy, and add your choice of flavourings. Add sultanas, raisins, toasted coconut flakes, or any other dried additions at the start of cooking, and stir in honey, cream, golden syrup, muscovado sugar, apple purée, home-made fruit syrup, chocolate sauce, chocolate chunks, or any other meltable or soluble trimming you can think of, when it's done.

Proper Gravy. Once your meat has finished roasting and you've lifted it onto a serving dish, transfer the roasting tin to the hob, having poured off almost all fat into a basin for use in frying etc. Then shake a little plain flour into the tin, and brown it carefully. Pour in about a gill (140ml) of hot water plus a stock cube, or just some rich home-made stock, and boil it, stirring all the time and scraping off the brown particles from the sides of the tin. Alternatively, the gravy can be thickened and browned with readymade granules, following directions on the packet. Season the gravy carefully and strain.

Fish Cakes. Leftover mashed potato can be turned into gorgeous fishcakes, providing a tasty meal for a matter of pence. Keep the cheapest possible smoked mackerel in the freezer ready. Thaw, skin and flake the mackerel, blend into the mash, and form into cakes before drying. If the mash is too soft to hold its shape, a little instant mashed potato added dry, or some plain flour, will take up excess moisture. Stir this in thoroughly and leave for a couple of minutes to absorb before forming the cakes. Rolling the finished cakes in semolina or oatmeal before frying adds a stylish flourish. Serve with home-made fresh tartar sauce.

Fresh Tartar Sauce. Combine 1 finely chopped four-inch (10cm) gherkin, a tablespoonful chopped capers (or pickled nasturtium seeds), a teaspoonful mustard, and a teaspoonful creamed horseradish with about five tablespoonsful plain yoghurt or mayonnaise. Yoghurt is cheaper, healthier, and gives a fresh, tangy edge, making this ideal to accompany any fried fish recipe. Improves with standing, and will keep in the fridge for a couple of weeks.

Stewed Red Cabbage. With sausages or pork dishes of any kind, properly stewed red cabbage is a dream. Slice up a small red cabbage, wash, and put into a saucepan with pepper, salt, no water but what hangs about it, and a generous piece of butter. Stew til quite tender, then add a slug of cider vinegar, and cook for a few minutes longer. NB: A mound of mashed roast squash, and a little good mustard on the side of the plate, will elevate this dinner to ambrosial levels.

To Boil Tough Greens. Trim off the stalks and all discoloured leaves and wash the greens well in cold, salted water. Let them remain in clean, cold, salted water for twenty to thirty minutes, allowing two tablespoonfuls of salt to each quart of water. Have ready a pan of boiling, salted water. If the water is hard, add a tiny pinch of bicarbonate of soda. Put in the greens and boil them steadily with the lid off the pan for about ten to fifteen minutes until tender. Drain off the water through a colander – or in the case of sprouts, add a little butter or margerine and a dust of pepper, and serve them in a hot dish – but with all other greens, press them well, chop them finely, then add butter and pepper.

Gratin of Potato, Celeriac and Other 'Root' Vegetables. Old, unappealing, sprouty and wrinkled potatoes are transformed into a highlight of the meal if they are peeled, sliced thinly on the mandolin part of your grater, and laid in a generously buttered roasting tin for gratinating. Layering with celeriac, parsnips, or any other tasty, hard vegetable adds a twist to keep life interesting, and even plain this is just the thing to lift the spirits at the end of a dreary day. To about a pound of vegetables, mix up about ¾ pint (350ml) of milk with a couple of tablespoonsful of cream, a teaspoonful of flour, plus salt and pepper to taste. Sprinkle the top of the layered vegetables with crumbled cheese (old hard back-of-the-fridge cheese is perfect, whether plain or blue), maybe also grate over a little nutmeg, and then pour the milky mixture over the top. Bake at any temperature between 160° and 220°C for around half an hour, the time of course varying dependent on the temperature. You're aiming to have a delicious caramelised brown crust with soft, melt-in-the-mouth vegetables underneath. You can leave off the cheese, and you could also add mushrooms and/or onions to the vegetable mix. This is a really versatile way of making a treat out of practically nothing.

Roast Vegetables. Make fuel go further by filling the oven when it's on, and get as many meals as you can from what you've cooked in it. Squashes and root vegetables, lightly doused with olive oil and roasted in bulk with garlic, onion, and a little rosemary, can be had as a vegetable, then later in the week be mashed (reheat in a pan with butter and milk, and then mash), and finally whizzed up with 50/50 stock and milk to make a delicious soup.

Yorkshire Pudding. 8oz (250g) plain flour, 3 eggs, pinch of salt, and up to a pint of either whole milk or milk and water combined. Add the egg to the flour and salt, plus a little milk. Stir into a batter, then add milk until the mix is creamy and pourable. Heat oil or dripping in a roasting tin to 230°C (or as hot as you can go), pour the batter carefully into the hot oil, and return to the oven for around twenty minutes. Not only is Yorkshire pudding fantastic as an accompaniment to meat, it's also sensational eaten cold with jam!

Toad in the Hole. So cheap, so delicious. Have some ready-cooked sausages or chunks of leftover roast meat to hand (leftover meat chunks were in fact the original 'toads'). If you haven't enough sausages to go round, chop them into one-inch pieces and distribute evenly. Make up the Yorkshire pudding batter as above, heat the oil or dripping, and then pour just a very thin layer of batter into the tin, return to the oven for five minutes, then remove, lay the meat or sausages out over the surface, pour on the remaining batter, and return to the oven to cook for twenty minutes or so.

Semolina. To a pint of milk add 2oz ground semolina, and stir constantly while heating to boiling point. Turn down and simmer for a few minutes, adding sugar to taste. Remove from the heat and break an egg into it, stirring briskly. Sprinkle with nutmeg before serving. Gorgeous served over a layer of jam or potted fruit, and can be finished by baking for ten minutes if you're worried about the egg.

The Stock Pot

Stock is a liquid containing all the flavour and nutriment – extracted by boiling – of meat, bones, vegetables, or fish. It's at the heart of all the most delicious and nourishing Winter meals, and provides a perfect use for all manner of otherwise wasted food materials. Fat should be added with the meat and can be removed when the stock has become cold. And if you haven't yet constructed your haybox, then do hurry up! If you want to make delicious stock but don't want to use the fuel required to do it on the hob, the haybox is an absolutely essential piece of equipment.

Making your own stock is the secret key to producing restaurant-quality dishes. Even a basic gravy becomes a thing of beauty if made with proper stock. Make up big batches and then freeze in smaller volumes. The frozen lump of stock can be added straight to the pan at the appropriate stage in the middle of cooking. Simply lower the heat a little, and leave to melt gently until the base of the pan is covered with liquid, before raising the temperature to resume normal cooking.

Everyday Stock. If you're around the house full time, then it's practical to run an everyday stockpot. If you fit your kitchen duties around a busy schedule away from the home, then the best option is to make up the recipes below, and freeze them in meal-sized portions.

Management of an everyday stockpot takes you straight back to the way kitchens were run for centuries. Half-fill a stockpot or large saucepan with cold water and add a teaspoonful of salt. Collect all pieces of bone, meat, vegetable etc, add them, and let the pot simmer gently for five to six hours, adding suitable scraps from each meal. Rice and potatoes should not be added to the stock, since they are apt to become sour. Empty the pan each night, straining the contents into a clean basin. Next day, add more scraps to the strained stock. Skim the stock carefully before returning to the pan.

Chicken and Bacon Stock. One of the most delicious and economical stocks results from cooking a bacon hock alongside a chicken carcass. The hock is then drained and the meat used as ham (it can even be honeyed and roasted). Adjust the cooking time according to whether you want to slice the ham off the bone, or to have it succulently tender and falling apart in pieces. To a bacon hock and a carcass, add the flavourings as per 'classic chicken stock', below, plus any herbs you fancy – but never use parsley when boiling bacon or ham, since it gives a really odd flavour. Again, the flesh from the cooked chicken bones can be used to make soup, and a little of the meat from the hock being added to this creates a delicious 'chicken and ham' classic. Only add salt at the end of cooking, and taste carefully before adding, since the bacon could already make the stock salty enough. Strain, cool and freeze as before.

Classic Beef Stock. To make six pints (3 litres) of good beef stock, put two pounds (1kg) fresh shin of beef, ½lb (250g) bones, broken up, plus 7 pints (3½ litres) water, into a pan and slowly raise to the boil. Skim frequently, and from time to time add a little cold water since this helps the scum to rise to the top. Once the stock has been skimmed well, add 1oz (25g) salt, one onion (with one or two cloves stuck into it), a stick of celery, a quartered turnip, a sliced carrot, a sliced parsnip, and a teaspoonful of whole peppercorns. Simmer at 180° to 200°F (80° to 90°C) for four or five hours. Strain off, leave to go cold, remove fat, and freeze.

Classic Chicken Stock. Take one fresh chicken carcass (available from any proper butcher), add a sliced carrot, a stick of celery, a small onion (or a leek), a bay leaf or two and half a teaspoonful of peppercorns. Cover with water, bring to the boil, and then simmer for four or five hours, or leave to cook overnight in the haybox. Strain, add salt to taste, leave to cool, and then freeze. One carcass should produce about 3 pints rich stock, depending on the size of your pan. The cooked flesh can be removed from the bones for curry or soup.

Pheasant and Pumpkin Stock. In the Autumn, if your butcher also deals in game, they are likely to have a mountain of pheasant carcasses to get rid of. The oddly sweet flavour of pheasant can be hard to manage, but if the carcasses are had when they are barely hung, and if the seeds and surrounding stringy flesh from a pumpkin, squash or two, are added, the stock to be had can be sublimely delicious. The flesh will drop easily from the bones after cooking, making a soup or curry made from the discarded parts of pheasants the perfect way to get maximum value from a sometimes awkward bird.

Fish Stock. Only flavoursome fish should be used. This Edwardian recipe yields a delicious stock best used fresh for fish soups or fish pie sauce. Take 1lb (500g) skate, four or five flounders, and two pounds (1kg) eels. Clean them well and cut them into pieces, cover them with water, and season with mace, pepper, salt, an onion stuck with cloves, a stick of celery, two sliced parsley roots (or some parsley leaves), and a bunch of herbs (tarragon, dill, bay and thyme will all go well). Simmer, covered, for an hour and a half, then strain off for use. You could of course use trimmings begged from the fishmonger for this.

Cold Meats

Meat prepared for eating cold should be gently boiled, leaving it far more succulent than roasting. Chicken and turkey can be simply boiled, skinned and sliced. Ham and beef can be further processed to make something really special, whether by salting before cooking, or by slow roasting afterwards. Reuse the cooking water to make a rich stock, or as a thin stock in its own right, for gravy, soup etc.

Roast Ham. A full-sized ham, or a bacon hock, boiled as described above and with the skin removed but a little fat left in place, can next be studded with cloves, painted with honey, or maybe coated with molasses and coarsely ground pepper, and then roasted to create beautiful ham for special occasions or for putting into sandwiches.

Salt Beef. One pound (500g) brisket is rubbed with 2oz (50g) salt, 1oz (25g) coarse sugar, 10 bay leaves crumbled and then ground up with 1 tablespoon salt, plus 1 tablespoonful saltpetre (potassium nitrate). Rub and turn every day for two weeks, and then boil slowly until tender, drain, and weight down until cold. This is most practical to do in large batches and then hang in the larder to store.

Stews and Pies

Stewing is the basis of what are called 'made dishes', including pies, and possesses over other methods of cooking the advantage of rendering tender even the toughest and coarsest meat. The perfection of stewing depends on the slow process by which the cooking is accomplished. Great haste in all matters generally signifies less speed; in this case it means no speed at all, but rather absolute failure. Stewing is essentially gently slow cooking in liquid, in a covered pan. Remove the lid as little as possible during cooking. Indeed, if cooking on the hob or in the oven, shake the pot from time to time rather than stirring.

Using a haybox is by far the most economical and successful method of producing a delicious stew. Add either cooked potatoes, instant mash, cornflour (this first mixed with a little cold water, vinegar or red wine), or plain flour to thicken the sauce once all the ingredients are thoroughly cooked. Pork stews are made delicious by the addition of a few chopped prunes; venison, rabbit or mixed game stews benefit from two or three crushed juniper berries; and all stews become seriously fantastic if you stir in a teaspoonful of molasses towards the end of cooking.

Irish Stew. Scrag end, mutton, or any inferior pieces of meat, may be made into an Irish stew. Trim off most of the fat, and cut into as many cutlets as you have bones; shape them and sprinkle with pepper. Peel six moderate sized onions, and for every pound of meat take one pound of potatoes. Blanch or parboil the vegetables separately, and cut them into slices. Take a clean six-pint (3 litre) stewpan, and add half a pint (250ml) water or stock. Arrange a layer of potatoes at the bottom of the pan, then a layer of meat, then onions, then potatoes, then meat, then onions, and finish the top with a good layer of potatoes. A rasher or two of bacon or ham is a valuable addition. Stew very slowly til the meat is done. Have sufficient stock or water, and add as required to prevent burning. A perfect haybox dinner, prepared at bedtime the night before it's needed.

Meat or Vegetable Pies. Cold leftover stew makes a fabulous pie filling, so make extra, maybe thicken it a little further, and then freeze in portions of a size suitable for making quick and easy home-made pies. All you have to do then is remember to thaw the filling(!), knock up some pastry, make the pie and throw it into the oven at 180°C for twenty minutes or so. A suet crust makes an interesting change from pastry. An alternative, and ideal for quick, delicious chicken pies, is to freeze a thick chicken stock-based soup and use this as a sauce over fried, braised or boiled fillings (such as chicken with mushrooms, leeks, ham etc).

Suet Crust. 1lb (500g) self-raising flour, ½lb (250g) suet, ½tsp salt, cold water. Mix together flour, salt, and suet, then mix into a soft dough with cold water. The addition of a generous quantity of mixed chopped fresh herbs (sage, oregano, marjoram, rosemary, etc) and/or a teaspoonful of creamed horseradish makes a delicious topping for steak and kidney or other strong meat fillings.

Soups

In the face of all the horrid tinned and packet products manufacturers have pumped out during the past few years (many of which were, ultimately, little more than flavouring and a bit of thickener), soup seems to have lost its deserving place as a hearty and sustaining meal in a bowl. Accompanied by some really good home-made bread, a thick, nourishing home-made soup can easily stand as lunch – or even, if you have a big enough chunk of bread, a whole supper. The basis of all soup is a sound stock.

Carrot Soup. Two pints (I litre) stock, one pint (500ml) of chopped or grated carrot, one chopped onion, 1oz (25g) butter or dripping, 1 tablespoonful cornflour, ½ teaspoon sugar, salt, pepper, nutmeg if liked. Melt the fat in a saucepan, add the carrot and onion and cook for a few minutes without browning. Add stock; boil gently until carrots are tender. Rub through a sieve or use a blender, re-boil it, and add the cornflour, mixed to a smooth paste with a little cold water. Stir the soup until it boils, then boil gently for fifteen minutes. To make carrot and coriander soup, add a good handful of finely chopped leaf coriander (fresh or frozen) right at the end of cooking. Skim carefully. Add the sugar and seasoning to taste, and serve in a hot tureen.

Tomato Soup. Two pints (I litre) stock, one pound (500g) tinned tomatoes or two pounds of sliced fresh tomatoes, 2 tablespoons chopped ham or bacon, 1oz (25g) dripping, small piece each of carrot, turnip and celery; one onion, parsley and other herbs to taste, 1 tsp sugar, heaped tablespoonful cornflour, salt and pepper. Cut up the vegetables (except the tomatoes) into small pieces. Melt the dripping, add the bacon, vegetables, parsley and herbs, and stir for ten minutes. Add the tomatoes, cook for about ten minutes, then add the stock and cook gently until the vegetables are soft. Remove the herbs and rub the rest through a sieve or use a blender. Reboil, and thicken with the cornflour, mixed to a smooth paste with a little cold water. Let it boil for five to ten minutes. Add the sugar, season carefully, and serve. If the tomatoes are very juicy, add more cornflour, as the soup should be the consistency of cream.

Cream of Brassica Soup. Two pints (1 litre) stock, 1lb (500g) brussels sprouts, dark green cabbage, or kale, 2 teaspoonsful cornflour, 2 floz (70ml) evaporated milk or double cream. Put the cooked brassicas through a sieve or blender, and add them to the stock with the cornflour, this first mixed to a smooth paste with a little cold stock. Let the soup boil well. Season carefully, add the cream or evaporated milk, and serve in a hot tureen with croutons of bread and maybe a sprinkle of nutmeg. Use a really good stock (chicken and bacon is perfect), and the soup will be quite delicious.

Thisandthat Soup. Any leftovers, including assorted vegetables, old cheese, meat scraps, bread, cold buttered toast, potato, rice etc, can be boiled up in stock and then whizzed in a blender to make soup. The success of this dish will depend on your skill in combining the scraps and in seasoning it, so maybe try a couple of the recipes first!

Sauces

Dry, tasteless, low nutrient and even over-the-hill foods can be turned into something quite special and sustaining by the addition of a carefully designed sauce. You can adapt basic sauces to enliven dried-out reheated meals, and to produce pasta dinners, cheesy comfort suppers, and even pizzas. Bought sauces, with their cheap ingredients, nutritionally useless thickeners, and priced-in wages and transport costs, can't compete with home-made versions, in terms of either food value or the flavour that makes life worth living.

White Sauce. The Basic Sauce: 1oz (25g) butter or margarine, 1oz plain flour, ½ pint (250ml) milk and water or stock, salt and pepper to taste. Melt the butter in a saucepan. Stir in the flour, add the liquid gradually, and stir until it boils. Let it simmer for ten minutes, then season and finish with the following additions; or just serve.

Parsley Sauce: Add a teaspoonful of chopped parsley.

Caper Sauce: Add a tablespoonful of chopped capers or pickled nasturtium seeds.

Egg Sauce: Add one hard-boiled egg, chopped.

Sweet Sauce: Add a tablespoonful of sugar and no pepper.

Onion Sauce: Add a few spoonfuls of chopped boiled onion.

Cheese Sauce: Parmesan rinds and back-of-the-fridge cheese (with any mould cut off) make the best cheese sauce. Sour milk used to make the main sauce will give this incredible flavour. Adding a teaspoonful of wholegrain mustard makes it *special*.

Brown Sauce. 1 pint (500ml) brown stock, 2 tablespoonfuls of plain flour, 1oz (25g) dripping or margarine, a sliced onion, a sliced carrot, parsley and herbs, salt, pepper, lemon juice. Melt fat in a pan, add vegetables, herbs, and flour, and fry them a light brown. Pour in the stock and stir til it boils. Season carefully, add a few drops of lemon juice, and let it simmer for fifteen minutes. Skim well and strain.

Tomato Sauce. 1lb (500g) sliced fresh tomatoes or a can, 1oz (25g) margarine, hard fat or olive oil, 1oz cornflour, an onion, chopped, some scraps of ham or bacon, garlic, herbs (basil being the obvious choice), 1 pint (500ml) stock or water, salt and pepper. Melt the fat in a pan, add the onion, garlic, ham, and herbs, and fry gently for ten minutes. Put in the tomatoes, add the stock or water, and the cornflour (mixed smoothly with a little cold water). Simmer the sauce gently from ten to fifteen minutes. Season carefully and blend or sieve. Reduce the water or stock you add to a minimum if this sauce is to be used for pizza or pasta.

Puddings

Fruit Yoghurt. Stir in some of your bottled cherries, damsons or plums, plus fruit syrup (either specially made, or from the jar) to taste. Much cheaper than those tiny bought plastic pots – and you can serve up as much as you want, too!

Sweet Omelettes. Add vanilla and a tablespoonful of sugar to the eggs. When the mixture is just setting, draw it to the handle side of the pan, press in the centre, put a little jam in the hollow and fold the mixture neatly over. Turn it upside down on a hot dish and dust with caster sugar.

Fruit Salad. Two bananas (sliced), half a tin of apricot halves, 4 tablespoonsful chopped tinned pineapple, one orange, 12 grapes, juice of one lemon, 2 gills (280ml) syrup from the fruit tins, 1 gill (140ml) water or orange juice, 3 or 4 ounces (around 100g) sugar. Boil the water/juice, syrup and sugar until a thin thread will form between the finger and thumb. Let it get cold, then add the lemon juice. Prepare the fruit and arrange it in a bowl, pour over the syrup, and mix all well together.

Basic Baked or Steamed Pudding. Two fresh eggs, and their weight in each self-raising flour, sugar, and butter or margarine, plus about a tablespoonful of milk. Beat the butter and sugar to a cream. Add the eggs one by one, beating them well in. Add the flour, blending lightly into the other ingredients. Lastly, add the milk, then either:

Turn the mixture into a greased basin, steam it for about an hour and serve with jam, or with margerine and brown sugar, or...

Put it in a greased pie-dish and bake until it is set and the top is nicely coloured, or... add about two tablespoonsful of grated chocolate and either steam or bake, or... line a pie-dish or deep plate with pastry. Put in a layer of jam, cover with some of the mixture, and bake carefully. Adding a little almond essence to the pudding mix even makes this into a passable 'Bakewell', or... grease some small dariole moulds or cups, cover the bottom with cleaned currants, half fill with pudding mixture, and steam or bake until set. Turn out very carefully, or... add marmalade or jam to the mixture and steam it.

Queen Pudding. 2oz (50g) white breadcrumbs or cake crumbs, ½ pint of milk, thinly pared rind of a lemon, 3oz (75g) sugar, 1oz butter or margarine, 2 fresh eggs, jam or ready-to-eat dried fruit. Put the milk in a pan with the thinly pared lemon rind and bring it to the boil. Then strain out the rind and put the milk back in the pan. Add the butter, crumbs, and one ounce of sugar and let these cook for a few minutes. Let the mixture cool slightly, then add the beaten yolks of the eggs and stir them in. Put the mixture in a greased fireproof dish and bake until pale brown. Put a thick layer of jam or stewed fruit on top. Next, whisk the whites of the two eggs to a stiff froth, stir in the rest of the sugar very lightly, and heap this meringue over the pudding. Put it in a cool oven until the meringue is crisp and a pretty biscuit tint. A few glacé cherries may be added if liked.

Treacle Sponge. ½lb (250g) self-raising flour, ¼lb (125g) suet, ¾oz (15-20g) ground ginger, ¼ pint milk, I egg, one gill (140ml) golden syrup. Sieve the flour, sugar and ginger into a basin. Add the suet. Beat up the egg. Mix the syrup and milk with it and stir this into the mixture in the basin, adding more milk if required as the mixture should be fairly moist. Have ready a greased pudding-basin, put in the mixture, cover the top of the basin with a piece of greased paper. Put it in a pan with boiling water to come half-way up the basin and steam for two hours (or use the haybox). Serve with sweet white sauce or heated syrup with a squeeze of lemon juice in it.

Apple Amber. About a pound of apples weighed after they are peeled and cored, 3oz (75g) caster sugar, rind of a lemon, 3 eggs, pastry. Peel, core, and slice the apples, put them in a pan with the sugar, lemon rind, and just enough water to keep them from burning. Let them stew gently until they are tender, then rub them through a sieve or mash them smoothly. Line round the edge and an inch or so down the side of a pie-dish with pastry, also stamp it into small rounds with a fluted cutter, brush one side of each with a little water, and arrange them slightly over-lapping each other on the pastry round the edge of the dish. Separate the eggs, beat up the yolks and stir them into the sieved apple, then pour the mixture into the prepared dish and bake in a moderate oven. Whisk the whites of the eggs to a stiff froth, stir about three tablespoonfuls of caster sugar lightly into them, then pile this meringue lightly over the apple mixture, sprinkling it with caster sugar. Set in a slow oven, until the meringue is set.

Apple or Elderflower Fritters. Firm eating apples, peeled, cored and thickly sliced, or elderflowers on the stem, washed. 4oz (125g) flour, 2 eggs, I tablespoonful oil or ghee (clarified butter), up to ½ pint (250ml) milk, sugar. Sprinkle the apples with sugar and leave several hours or overnight. Drain well. Heat a pan of oil ready for frying. Mix together the flour, one whole egg, the yolk of the second egg, and the oil/ghee. Beat in about half the milk and then add more until the batter has a creamy dropping consistency. Finally, whisk the second egg white until in stiff peaks, and then fold this into the batter. Dip the apple slices or elderflowers into the batter, coating evenly, and then drop into the hot oil to fry until golden brown. Serve straight away, sprinkled with sugar and maybe a little cinnamon.

A Very Superior Trifle. Makes enough for eight, and is fabulous enough for celebrations. Stale cake (made up to volume if necessary with macaroons, amaretti, or boudoir biscuits), some flavoursome booze from assorted near-empty bottles, 1 pint single cream, 2 large egg yolks, 2 large eggs, 1 tablespoon ground rice or flour, caster sugar, raspberry jam or other fruit preserve. Topping: 8 tablespoons white wine or sherry, rind and juice of a lemon, 2oz (50g) sugar, ½ pint (250ml) double cream, nutmeg. *Method:* Put the cake in the bottom of a big serving dish and pour on the alcohol. Leave to soak, and check from time to time, adding more booze until the cake is soaked and soft. Topping: put the wine and lemon juice into a bowl, stir in the sugar until dissolved, then, still stirring, pour the cream in slowly. Add a little grated nutmeg, then whisk until it holds its shape. Don't over-whisk or it could curdle. Next make the custard. Beat the egg yolks and whole eggs together with the ground rice or flour, then bring the single cream to the boil, and pour it on to the eggs. Return the mixture to the pan and cook gently without boiling until very thick, stirring constantly with a wooden or silicone spoon. Season with sugar to taste, then pour over the cake and leave in a cool place to set. When firm, spread with a layer of jam, add the topping, and decorate as required. Leave overnight before serving, preferably in a cool larder rather than fridge, since this helps the flavours to develop.

4: BAKING BASICS

Baking is a massive and popular subject, with plenty of books devoted to it. Here I'm just going to give you the basic tools you'll need to save both time and money...

Five Top Tips

1) Use sour milk to make cakes or scones. It actually makes them lighter and more delicious.

2) One teaspoonful of glycerine per pound of flour makes cakes much lighter and sweeter – more like 'bought', if you like that sort of thing.

3) Measuring syrup or other sticky material is made more economical if you dip the measure in boiling water before use. This prevents the syrup from sticking, so none ends up in the washing-up water.

4) To weigh sticky stuff or baking fat, sprinkle a little flour in the scale pan.

5) When making a cake, weigh the sugar first, then weigh the fat on top of it. This way the fat will slide into the mixing bowl for creaming without leaving a trace in the scalepan, which can then be cleaned with a quick wipe out over the sink.

Pastry

If you can make pastry, your kitchen becomes the source of just about anything your tastebuds might desire, from sustaining meat pies to an indulgent Danish. Here are the various types of pastry you might need in everyday life. Have your hands and equipment as cold as possible, handle the pastry as little as possible, and only ever add the bare minimum of water. Always rest your pastry in the fridge for around twenty minutes, wrapped in plastic or covered with a damp cloth, before attempting to roll it out. This helps the proteins to develop, making it stretchy. Not resting it properly will only convince you that you can't make pastry at all...

   Short Crust Pastry. The easy multipurpose pastry. *Ingredients:* Ilb (500g) plain flour, ½lb (250g) margarine or baking fat, a tablespoonful baking powder, ¼ teaspoonful salt, cold water.

Method: Mix together the flour, baking powder and salt. If the fat is hard, cut it into thin pieces before rubbing it into the flour. When the mixed flour and fat resemble breadcrumbs, make a well in the centre, pour in cold water, and mix the whole to a smooth, stiff paste. Knead it thoroughly but lightly. Roll it out on a floured board to the desired thickness. It can be used for most dishes when a good, plain crust is desired, such as pies, tarts, patties, tartlets etc.

Flaky Pastry. Delicious, slightly more involved pastry for Eccles cakes, etc. *Ingredients:* 1lb (500g) plain flour, ¾lb (350g) butter or baking fat, 1 tsp lemon juice, ¼ teaspoonful salt, cold water.

Method: Sieve the flour and salt together. Divide the butter into four pieces. Rub one-fourth of it into the flour, then mix to a stiff paste with the lemon juice and cold water (the paste should not be in the least wet). Turn it on to a floured board, knead it until it is smooth and free from cracks, then roll it out into a long strip barely a quarter of an inch thick. Work the butter on a plate then put it in little lumps in rows down the strips of pastry, leaving a narrow margin free round the edge. Sprinkle a little flour over the butter, fold the pastry in three, press the edges firmly together, and roll it out again into a long strip. Take the third portion of butter and treat it in the same way, and do the same

with the fourth portion. The pastry is now ready for use.

Bread

Before the invention of the nefarious Chorleywood Process in the 1960s, which enabled near-instant industrial production of a spongy, steamed bread-like product at low cost and big margins, bread used to be known as 'the staff of life'. You couldn't easily survive on that gluey supermarket sponge the factories make, though.

Proper fermented wholemeal bread, however, has a rightful place at the heart of anyone's diet; and if you make your own, you can enjoy the fanciest, most nutritious deli-style bread for less than the cost of a bag of factory sponge. Here I'll share just the archetypical British home wholemeal recipe, plus my own favourite seedy half-wholemeal recipe. Points to remember are that the longer it's risen the more tasty it becomes, best rising takes place at around 40°C, the more it's kneaded the better the crumb, add the liquid a little at a time, and if you accidentally make the dough too wet you can add more flour without problems. Again, there are plenty of books devoted to this vast and addictive subject, but I'm thrilled if I can be of service in getting you started...

The Grant Loaf. Doris Grant's 1944 recipe is the origin of most home-made bread recipes, and is quick and easy to do since it's only kneaded and risen once. Makes 3lb bread.

Ingredients: 3lb (1.5kg) stoneground wholemeal flour, 2 tsp salt, 2 pints (1 litre) water at blood-heat, 1 tablespoon sugar, molasses or honey, 1 tablespoon dried yeast.

Method: Sprinkle the yeast into a little of the water to start working, and keep warm. Weigh out the flour and add the salt. Once the yeast has started to produce little islands on the top of the water, stir in the sugar or molasses. After about fifteen minutes the yeast should be ready to add to the flour. Mix well (by hand is best), and as you mix, add the rest of the water a little at a time, plus a little more if needed, and then carry on kneading until the dough feels elastic and comes away from the sides of the mixing bowl cleanly. Divide into the greased and warmed tins, put in a warm place covered with a damp cloth or plastic bag, and leave until the dough has risen to within around half an inch (1.5cm) of the top of the tins. Bake at around 200°C (gas mark 6) for 35 to 40 minutes.

The Leavey Loaf! This is a modified and super-nutritious version of the bread my mother used to make when we were children, and I'm still not tired of it. I use organic wholemeal and non-organic white flour, since this way the bran is pesticide-free, and the crumb is very much lighter. If you substitute rye flour for most of the wholemeal, and sprinkle in half a teaspoon of caraway seeds, you get an unusually fragrant and interesting copycat of a traditional sourdough loaf.

Ingredients: 1lb (500g) stoneground organic wholemeal flour, 1lb strong plain white flour, 1 or 2 tablespoons molasses or treacle, 1 pint (500ml) water, 1 or 2 tablespoons sunflower oil, 1 tsp salt, 1oz (25g) each golden linseed, sunflower seeds, sesame seeds, 1 tsp yeast.

Method: Put the molasses in a measuring jug and add about half a pint boiling water to dissolve. Top up to the correct amount with cold water; leave to cool if necessary (if you can hold your finger in the liquid without flinching it's good), then sprinkle in the yeast. Keep warm until foaming nicely and the islands are forming on the surface. Combine the flours and salt and rub the sunflower oil into the mixture. Add your choice of seeds. Pour in the yeast mix when it's ready, a little at a time, mixing thoroughly by hand all the while, and discard any surplus liquid once the dough is springy, stretchy, and comes away cleanly from the bowl. Knead for another five minutes or so, then cover with a damp cloth or plastic bag and leave in a warm place until doubled in size. Oil a 2lb loaf tin and re-knead the dough in the bowl before pressing it down into the tin. This process is called 'knocking back'. Cover once more and leave to rise until the bread is almost level with the top edge of the tin. Put into a cold oven and heat to 180°C (gas mark 4), then after twenty minutes turn down to 160°C (mark 3) for another twenty minutes or so. Tap on the top of the loaf, and if you get a hollow sound the bread is ready. Leave standing on the cooling rack in the tin for a few minutes, and it will draw away from the sides, making it easier to turn out to finish cooling.

Easy Treats

And finally, here are a couple of easy, delicious sweet treats for throwing together. Emergency presents, happy kids!

Pure Butter Shortbread.

Regardless of the salty stuff you can buy quite cheaply, proper home-made shortbread still makes a super present.

Ingredients: ¼lb (125g) plain flour, 2½oz (65g) salted butter, 1oz (25g) caster sugar.

Method: Rub the butter into the flour and sugar lightly at first, then use more pressure until the butter begins to bind the flour. Turn the paste on to a floured board and knead the mixture until it no longer crumbles, but is a soft, pliable paste – the length of time it takes will depend on the weather and the heat of the room. Use no moisture of any kind. Roll out the paste about three-quarters of an inch thick. Using a fork, crimp the edge, and prick the surface all over, pressing right through the thickness of paste. Bake very slowly for about ¾ hour.

A Good All-Purpose Cake.

This basic but rich recipe can be adapted by throwing in some of the flavourings listed below to add variety without research or fuss.

Ingredients: 12oz (300g) self-raising flour, 8oz (200g) butter, margarine or baking fat, 8oz sugar, 5 eggs, 6 tablespoonsful milk, grated rind of one lemon.

Method: Sieve the flour. Cream the butter and sugar. Beat the eggs, one by one, into the butter and sugar, and lightly fold in the flour and lemon rind. Add the milk. Pour the mixture into a paper-lined cake tin, and bake in a moderately hot oven for about one and a half hours.

Fruit Cake. Once the flour is added, add a cup each of currants and sultanas, and four tablespoons chopped peel (if liked).

Seed cake. Add about an ounce of caraway seeds.

Sultana Cake. Add a cup of sultanas and a little chopped peel.

Pineapple Cake. Add five tablespoons tinned pineapple pieces, and substitute four tablespoons of the syrup in place of the milk. Also leave out the lemon rind.

Banana cake. Mash two over-ripe bananas and stir them into the mixture. Leave out three eggs, and the lemon rind.

5: VALUE, ADDED

'Value Added' is a business term for taking raw materials and, with a little effort and ingenuity, transforming them into something with a retail value many times the original cost. Here are one or two unexpected activities which will make your kitchen the thriftiest place on the planet...

Feeding Animals

Keeping animals can be expensive, so it's good to know that you can minimise the cost by cooking up delicious meals for your pets.

Chickens will eat peelings and cooked scraps greedily. You can also boil up a decent **Mash for Hens**. Use the water poured off from boiling vegetables to boil up all the peelings and food waste, including leftover bread, stale breakfast cereal, cake, biscuits, cooked rice and pasta, and even scraps of cooked meat, then feed the mash to the chickens alongside their usual pellets. And if you scrape up the chickens' 'non-egg product' and put it in the compost heap you'll be using the nutrients a second time over, via your veg crops.

Fat Balls for Wild Birds are a pricy luxury which can be happily produced in the home, and for nothing if you're smart about it. If you can find a source of packet lard (butchers sometimes sell it), this is convenient and easy – but to save money, collect up fat that's dripped from beef and lamb, then melt it slowly in a bain marie, and stir in seeds and grains. Growing ornamental millet and sunflowers is the obvious way to ensure a free supply.

Dogs, like chickens, can be fed scraps cooked up into a porridgy mixture. Brown rice and rolled oats are both good base ingredients for a **Dog's Mash**, and a spoonful of molasses will give lots of trace elements too. By the way, you'll save hugely on tyres and fuel if you give your dog dried feed, softened with a touch of hot water, rather than lugging about the dead weight of wet food in cans. Offal, such as hearts, livers, brains, lights (lungs) and tripe (stomach), is all available very cheaply from any proper butcher's – and dogs, to their credit, love that sort of thing.

Cats are very partial to a bit of fish, so in addition to trying them with the offal listed above for dogs (which a fussy cat may well scorn), ask at your local chippy if they have any trimmings you could take off their hands. Cook it gently, add gelatine to the liquor to make a jelly, and bag in small volumes for the freezer. The chip shop owner will save on expensive disposal, you'll be saving hugely – and the cat will be smiling in a distinctly Cheshire style, too!

The Self Preservation Society

You don't need to have a big garden or allotment surplus to find preserving a useful money-saving technique. Some things flood the shops from time to time – and if you can take advantage of this by storing the bounty, you'll not only be saving future outlay, but you'll also, weirdly, and in a very small way, be playing the futures market too! And it goes without saying that in Winter, shop prices for fresh produce rise – and your preserved foods suddenly become even better value than they were when you made them.

I'm afraid you won't find me telling you here how to bottle a 3lb cockerel, or how to tin a tongue; even though my best book on the topic does indeed give full and careful instructions. I've no doubt I'd end up making you very ill if I were to attempt to share this kind of high-falutin' alchemy in anything other than full detail.

Drying

A ridiculous amount of money may be saved simply by producing your own herbs. They will taste better – and will store longer, too. There are two simple but essential rules for successfully producing a superior quality cold-dried product. First, the leaves must be kept as cool as possible while they are drying, and second they must be kept – as far as possible – in the dark. Beyond those rules there are guidelines, but guidelines worth observing nonetheless. Pick your material as early in the morning as you can, as soon as the dew has dried, on a bright, dry, but not hot day. Get rid of any brown or damaged leaves, then gather the stems neatly together and tie as tightly as you can. Pick a location where the bunches can be hung upside down in cool, dry moving air. An airing cupboard is pretty much the worst place you could possibly choose, by the way, since the warmth will drive off the volatile aromatic compounds. If you can't find anywhere dark enough, tie the leaves inside a paper bag. A bag is also useful if you are drying seedheads, whether for next year's planting or (with caraway, fennel, poppies, sunflowers, linseed, millet etc) for use in food. Pack dried leaves whole into airtight containers, and crumble only when used. Shake seed heads hard (bashing if necessary), still inside their bag, and the seeds can then be poured straight from there into a container.

Herbs suited to drying include mint, sage, rosemary, lemon verbena and chamomile (for chamomile, collect the flower heads only, pack very loosely in a paper bag, and shake frequently). The delicate and watery basil, coriander and parsley are better frozen.

Apple rings, pears, plums, runner beans, and all sorts of other vegetables may be dried, though the majority need special preparation so won't be dealt with in detail here. In damp Britain, warmth will be needed. Underneath a woodburner is an excellent place, the material spread on muslin on a rack to ensure good air circulation. Mushrooms, however, can be very successfully dried without preparation, as long as they're kept cool. If you have a big darning needle, they can be threaded into strings and hung up to dry. Soak to soften when using.

Pickling

Pickling is quick and easy, and light on fuel. Ready-spiced vinegar designed for onions, gherkins, cauliflower etc, still appears in all good greengrocers at the right time of year. Onions, gherkins, young walnuts, pears, plums, red cabbage, nasturtium seeds, cauliflower florets – and even hard-boiled eggs – can be readily pickled. Vegetables and walnuts should be salted or left to soak in brine for at least twenty-four hours, then thoroughly drained and patted dry. Pack the items to be pickled tightly into jars and cover them in cold vinegar. There are of course many small variations to the method and ingredients, depending on what it is you're pickling, but overall, it really is as simple as that!

Pickled Nasturtium Seeds. Nasturtium seeds, pickled and stored for a little while to mature, make a tasty substitute for expensive capers. Perfect for use in home-made pasta sauces, on pizzas, or in tartar sauce for consuming with fish. Keep the seeds for a few days after they are gathered, then pour boiling vinegar over them. Once cold, put into jars and cover. They will not be fit to eat for some months, but are then finely flavoured, and by many are preferred.

Sweet Fruit Preserves

Jams, jellies, marmalades, cheeses and butters are fruit preserves of undoubted merit. They are particularly rich in energy-giving foods, and possess considerable value as internal cleansers. Home-made jams are every whit equal to the commercial preserves and in many cases infinitely superior. Old bought jars which maybe don't seal so well can be reused for boiled fruit preserves pretty much *ad infinitum*, though it makes sense to reserve the oldest jars for preserves that are boiled long and hot, or contain more than 50% sugar.

To Preserve Fresh Raspberries without Boiling. Perfect if the only raspberries you get to see are in supermarket punnets. Weigh an equal quantity of fruit and sugar. Bruise the fruit and add the sugar, ground up in the food processor to a powder, or use icing sugar. Let it stand for two hours, til the sugar is diffused, and mixed well with the fruit. Put into small jars, cover with ghee (clarified butter), and lid tightly. Use small jars and use up quickly once opened. Useful for adding to yoghurt, sponge puddings, layering cakes etc, or just eating, secretly, behind the pantry door.

Syrups. Home-made fruit syrups can be used to make delicious hot or cold drinks, puddings (blancmange, fool, jelly, cheesecake topping, fruit yoghurt), and as general flavourings (eg. poured over ice cream, in a syllabub, or incorporated into a sponge cake for extra moistness and flavour). Blackcurrant, rosehip and elderberry syrups are fantastic high-vitamin Winter pick-me-ups, and super remedies for sore throats. You can take them straight from the spoon, or made up into a squash or tea. Blander fruits, such as apples, pears, plums and gooseberries are not really worth experimenting with.

Syrups are very simply made, and all follow similar lines. You'll need a pan or double boiler (not iron, zinc, copper, or chipped enamel, since contact with reactive metal will destroy the Vitamin C), a muslin cloth or jelly bag, wooden spoon, and suitable bottles. Lever-top bottles can be had from hardware stores, and since these have replaceable seals they are worth the investment, just to ensure that your precious gourmet syrup doesn't turn to mouldy soup thanks to a dodgy cap. First you very gently simmer the fruit down, pressing and stirring from time to time, so that the juice is expelled. Add about half a pint of water (250ml) to every two pounds (1kg) of fruit at the start of cooking. Lay a muslin sheet or jelly bag in a large bowl and decant the fruity mess into it, then hang up over the bowl overnight to strain out the juice.

To every pint (500ml) of the cold strained juice, add around ¾lb (350g) sugar, and stir until dissolved. This quantity can be adjusted according to your taste, though adding the maximum amount will help to preserve the syrup without significant loss of colour or taste. If you can't bear the faff of proper sterilising, syrups can be preserved for a while by adding a small glass of brandy for every pint of liquid, or by adding a little bit of a Camden tablet to each bottle, or by using the equipment described under 'bottling', below. To sterilise thoroughly, using heat, bottle and seal straight away, place in water bath so that the bottles are immersed right up to their necks, slowly heat to 170°F (75°C) over the course of about an hour, then keep the temperature at that level for 20 minutes for smaller bottles (up to about 250ml / ½ pint) or 30 minutes for larger. Do not allow to boil. Store cool and dark.

Jams and other boiled fruit preserves. Jam is such an easy way of putting surplus fruit down into store that everyone should make at least one jar during the course of their life, if only just to impress themselves with how clever they are! Wash and weigh the fruit, heat gently as for syrups until it's soft and mushy, then add 1lb of sugar for every pound of fruit you weighed at the start of the cooking. Put your jars into a cold oven and switch it on to heat them gently through (cold jars would shatter), then boil the jam hard until it turns dark and glassy, and test on a chilled saucer before packing into jars and sealing. Simple as that! A sugar thermometer makes judging when the jam is ready to pot very much easier, but the saucer test is foolproof: drop a little of the jam onto a chilled saucer, leave to cool for a moment and then push it with your finger. If it stays in a lump and the surface wrinkles, the jam is ready to pot.

The success of a jelly or jam depends not only on the skill and accuracy employed in making it. The pectin content of the fruit will largely determine how well it sets. Fleshy, high-pectin fruit like damsons, gooseberries and plums make super jams. Adding an apple or two, or a handful of gooseberries or redcurrants, to low-pectin fruits like strawberries or raspberries, or to any fruit that's rather riper than it should be, will also help with the setting. Strawberry jam is hard to make well, and jam-making, like drying vegetables, is a big subject; so I'll leave this topic with just one delicious and easy recipe to get you started. Damsons, by the way,

should never be gathered from field hedgerows without first asking permission. They're cultivated in the hedges, not growing wild, and may well be an important crop for the hard-pressed farmer.

Damson Jam. 1lb (500g) damsons, 1lb 2oz (550g) sugar, 2 floz (60ml) water. *Method:* Wash the damsons, and remove any mouldy fruit or rubbish. Put in a pan with the water and simmer for about half an hour, until the fruit is really soft. Add the sugar, stir until dissolved, and boil rapidly until setting point is reached, removing the stones with a slotted spoon as they rise to the surface. Will make about 2lb of the most delicious jam.

Jellies. Fruit jellies are, basically, syrups but made with more sugar, and with an eye to containing enough pectin to set them, making them thicker and spreadable. Delicious! The best fruits for setting a really good jelly are: crab apples, sour apples, blackberries, black, red or white currants, damsons, elderberries, gooseberries, greengages, lemons, limes, loganberries, quinces and sloes. All fruits with strong flavours, and high acid and pectin contents. Old jam jars are perfect for use in potting these, since the sealing of the lid is not critical.

Heat to extract the juice as for the syrups, then test the pectin content by putting a spoonful of the juice into an old container, then covering it with methylated spirit. If it forms one big lump there's plenty of pectin; a few largish lumps mean adequate pectin, and lots of small lumps mean not enough. You can add a few crab apples or gooseberries to the mix to remedy this, or you could also buy a pectin additive from cookshops, so all is not lost.

Strain the juice as for syrups, and leave overnight. Then add 1lb sugar (500g) to one pint (500ml) juice, and boil to setting point. You'll know this is near when the jelly darkens in colour and develops a super-transparent, glassy appearance. Test for setting by dropping a little of the jelly onto a chilled saucer. Leave for a moment to cool, then push with your finger. If it stays in a lump, and the surface wrinkles slightly, then it's ready to pot in pre-heated jars (see jam, below). Removing scum is recommended in the old books, but unless you're planning on entering any competitions I can't see much reason to agonise over this. Jellies in posh reused jars make very swanky presents.

Hedgerow Jelly. You'll need: 4lb (2kg) blackberries, 2lb (1kg) elderberries, 2lb (1kg) rosehips, 1lb (500g) wild apples or crab apples, plus sugar. Cut the crab apples in half and wash them and the rosehips, picking out any rubbish. Add the blackberries and elderberries. Place all in a saucepan, having just covered the bottom of the pan with water. Simmer until tender, stirring occasionally. Strain through fine jelly bag or muslin into a large bowl, and let stand all night. Weigh the liquid and return it to the saucepan, adding a pound (500g) of sugar for each pint (500ml) of juice. Bring quickly to the boil and boil briskly for fifteen to twenty minutes, until it sets when tested.

Bottling

Bottling is simple, cheap (it needn't cost anything at all), reliable and quick. Vegetables particularly suited to bottling include new potatoes, runner beans, green peas, broad beans, cauliflower, young carrots and asparagus. Invest in some specialist jars; you do sometimes find them at car boot sales, in which case, pounce! Replacement lids and seals are available, and be sure to buy a size that will fit inside your oven or pressure cooker! There are various jars available, the most popular being those with a removable rubber ring seal which can be replaced each time they're used for bottling. Weck make neat jars of a useful size, with spring clips to hold the lids on; Le Parfait is another popular brand, with a strong wire lever closure, and the screw-band Kilner jar is a British name we're thrilled to see back on the shelves after many years away. Recycle older seals on jars used for dry goods storage.

The critical process in bottling is the sterilising, during which the lid is also sealed down. The filled bottles are placed either into a water bath (deep enough to cover the jars up to the neck: a huge saucepan, enamel bread bin, pressure cooker, fish kettle, old Burco washboiler or similar), or into an oven. In the water bath a false bottom is needed. Pressure cookers and good quality fish kettles come with a raised base plate, though you can make one for any other vessel with a triple thickness of folded-over chicken wire, or alternatively, stand the jars on a few strips of narrow wood. Other equipment is a pair of heatproof, well-fitting gloves for lifting jars out of the hot steriliser, and a cooking thermometer.

Choosing and preparing fruit or vegetables for bottling is similar to preparing them for the freezer. Select only material that is in perfect condition, and fully ripe without tending to softness. Peel, core and slice apples; peel pears; remove the stones from plums and cherries; skin tomatoes and plums; and blanch beans and other vegetables. And if you object to brown colouration on your bottled fruit, you might also like to look into the exciting business of home sulphuring. Cooking the **Retro Metro** way is never tedious!

The prepared fruit and vegetables are closely packed, and then covered with either plain water, sugar syrup (¼lb / 125g sugar to one pint of water is a good multipurpose mix; for cherries, plums, pears etc), or salted water for vegetables. The exact method, temperature, and time taken for sterilising varies according to the product.

Chutneys

Chutneys are designed to give depth and piquancy to otherwise potentially tedious savoury dishes. Thrifty essentials, basically!

The equipment and technique are basically identical to those used for jam. The key differences are in the use of vinegar as a main ingredient, which means that the chutney is very well protected against spoiling, and in the fact that pectin levels and achieving the correct setting point are not critical to success. An added benefit is that you can use the lowest quality produce, including diseased, bruised, mouldy and dirty examples, and still come out with a delicious, high-quality product. Good candidates for chutney include: apples, blackberries, damsons, elderberries, gooseberries, plums, rhubarb, green and red tomatoes, marrow, beetroot, turnip, carrot and swede. You can sometimes get bananas ridiculously cheaply, and if so, indulging in the ecstasy of a good banana chutney is simply the only way to go. Incidentally, for flavour, plain brown malt vinegar and dark brown sugar (even muscovado if you can stand the extra cost) are the best choice for making really exciting chutneys.

The basic technique goes something like this: fruit and vegetables should be chopped or minced small, then placed in a pan with the spices, dried fruits, onions, garlic or other flavourings, and then just about covered with vinegar. Simmer gently in a closed pan until all the ingredients are soft. This could take from one to four hours, so using a haybox (see Chapter 2) for this stage is a great fuel-saving trick. Dissolve the sugar in the remaining vinegar, and add this to the pan, then, simmering gently with the lid off (haybox pans should at this point be moved back to the hob), stir thoroughly and often until the mixture thickens to your desired consistency. Pot at once into preheated jars (see under jam, above), and seal tightly.

Green tomato chutney is the classic recipe, making use of a crop which has usually only just begun to ripen when the first frosts descend. But not everybody can get hold of them, so instead here's a recipe for a rather tasty – and easy – marrow chutney, making use of something which arrives in bulk at the end of the Summer, and gets so cheap that I'm sure you've already seen them in the shops and puzzled over what you could possibly do with one if you actually bought it…

Marrow Chutney. 3lb (1.5kg) marrow (weight without skin or seeds), salt, ½lb (250g) shallots or mild onions (skinned and trimmed), ½lb apples (peeled and cored), 12 peppercorns, ¼oz (5-8g) dried whole root ginger (bruised by bashing), ½lb sultanas, 4oz (100g) sugar, 1½ pints (750ml) malt vinegar.

Because marrow is so watery, it's first salted as though it were going into a pickle. Also, because it's soft, there's no need for the separate covered long cooking process. Cut the marrow into small pieces, place in a bowl, and sprinkle generously with salt. Cover and leave for 12 hours. Drain well, and place in a pan with the sliced shallots and chopped apples. Tie the peppercorns and ginger into muslin, and add to the pan, along with the sultanas, sugar and vinegar. Bring to the boil, then reduce the heat to a simmer until the consistency is thick.

Table Sauces

Table sauces are basically liquified chutneys, and aside from the sieving, they're easy and quick. Ideal for those big boxes of over-ripe and damaged stuff that the greengrocer's anxious to get rid of – and the end result is a premium product that knocks all but the most expensive sauces into a cocked hat. Which could be messy.

Ripe tomatoes, plums, damsons, apples and elderberries all make delicious, high-nutrient sauces. Cook the fruit down until soft (the haybox is ideal for this), then sieve carefully. Add vinegar, spices, sugar and salt. Cook until the consistency is like thick cream, then pour at once into pre-heated bottles (see under jam for heating, and under syrups for the best bottles, both above) and seal immediately.

Wine, Beer and Liqueur Making

The easiest way of making delicious high-value alcoholic treats in your own kitchen is to make simple infused liqueurs. It's not the cheapest though, since by buying readymade alcohol you're paying a lot of tax. Buy cheap vodka, brandy or gin, then add sugar to taste, and pour over damsons, morello cherries, sloes, raspberries, blackcurrants or any other favourite fruit, and leave it to steep for a few months before draining and rebottling. The boozy fruit is actually preserved by this method, and makes an interesting ingredient for grown-up puddings.

Home brewing beer is where you start really saving, since at the time of writing, around $1/3$ of the cost of a pint bought in a British pub goes to the taxman. Brewing is also pretty simple, though it's messier and takes up a lot more space than the luxury liqueurs. It's easy to get into, too, with convenient kits of excellent quality now on the market at a very reasonable price. So get down to your local homebrew shop, buy a kit, make friends with the owner, and take this new and absorbing interest from there.

Home winemaking is an intense, science-heavy business – if you want it to be. It can also be a light-hearted one-gallon adventure, allowing for lots of creativity and excitement, as you wait for the bubbles to stop rising so you can at last taste that untried batch of 'Peapod and Parsnip 2013'! All you need to get started is flavouring materials, water, yeast and sugar, Camden tablets for sterilising, plus a one-gallon demijohn, a syphon tube, a large plastic lidded container, and an airlock. The rest of the equipment is already in your kitchen.

Beginners would do well to start off with crisp, fresh nettle wine, since it's simple, cheap, and, even if it becomes 'musty' (spoiled by the yeast), still tastes perfectly acceptable if you add lemonade!

Nettle Wine. ½ gallon (2 litres) young nettle tips, 4lb (1.8kg) sugar, 2 lemons, ½oz (10-15g) root ginger, 1 gallon (4.5 litres) water, general wine making yeast.

Rinse and drain the nettle tips, simmer in some of the water with the bruised ginger and the peel of the lemons, for 45 minutes or so (use the haybox to save fuel). Strain, and make up to a gallon with hot water. Pour over the sugar, stir until dissolved, then add the lemon juice and 1 tsp yeast. Keep the mix closely covered in a warm place for four days, stir thoroughly, and transfer to the demijohn. Fit the airlock, filled with water, and leave in the same warm place until it becomes clear, with a putty-coloured sediment in the bottom. Syphon off (or decant using a jug), leaving sediment behind as best you can, clean out the demijohn if you have only one, and set up once again to carry on fermenting until the bubbles stop rising. This should take about three months. Syphon again, into clean bottles, cork (tapered corks need no special tool), and store for nine months to a year before trying. If you can manage to wait that long.

Running a thrifty kitchen is not only about eking out the ingredients and fuel you're using in your cooking to gain maximum value. A bit of technical know-how will save even more money. Finding inventive uses for 'rubbish' is another way of turning waste into profit.

Bin Bags. Accept the odd plastic carrier bag here and there, and use these as free bin liners. Use the bag first for compost collecting, and again for any unrecyclable plastic that's heading for the dustbin. Everything else should be burnt, composted, repurposed, reused, or sent for recycling.

Bones. Fresh bones should be used to make stock. Bones stripped of cooked meat after stock making should be put in the fire and burnt to ash, then added to the compost heap or sprinkled around roses and fruit trees. They're a valuable source of potassium.

Butter. Gone-off butter can be revived for immediate use by covering it for an hour or two in fresh milk. Use at once. The milk can be used afterwards for making soup. Surplus fresh butter can be frozen.

Cheese. Old hard parmesan rinds will melt into cheese sauces completely. Any cheese that's old and hard makes delicious sauce, or topping for bakes. Simply cut off any mould (the origin of the term 'cheese paring'). Cheese can be protected from mould by keeping a lump of sugar in the container with it.

Citrus Fruits. Lemon rinds after squeezing make great brass or copper cleaners. Sprinkle salt into them and then rub over items to be cleaned, then rinse in warm soapy water and dry carefully. Roll lemons on the countertop before squeezing to make them yield more juice. For the maximum amount of juice per lemon, put them for a few minutes into very hot water, and they'll yield about twice the quantity. To peel citrus fruits cleanly, pour boiling water over them and leave them covered in the hot water for about five minutes.

Cleaning Products. Avoid brand names and avoid paying for some very expensive advertising! Have washing soda, bicarbonate of soda, methylated spirits and scouring powder to hand, and you should be able to tackle any everyday cleaning job. To hand-clean your oven, household ammonia is cheap (wear gloves). Pyrolytic electric ovens clean themselves economically if you run the program overnight on Economy Seven, though they are expensive to buy. Induction and ceramic hobs are cleaned beautifully by first scraping, then wiping over with a drop of washing-up liquid plus a little methylated spirits on a hot damp cloth. Buff off with a clean teatowel and it will shine like new. Bicarbonate of soda sprinkled onto a hot damp cloth makes a super stainless steel cleaner and general purpose surface cleaner. It's also very good for removing bad smells. Old pump bottles can be reused by filling with equal parts multipurpose cleaner concentrate and water. A solution of washing soda makes the cheapest grease-busting cleaner there is, and a strong solution can be used on tea and coffee stains, or (together with a piece of aluminium foil) for cleaning silver. 'Vim' or 'Ajax' scouring powders used on a hot damp cloth are super-cheap and excellent for all tough jobs, especially removing stains from enamel cookware, and cleaning tiles, worktops, and Belfast sinks.

Cloths. I use cheap heavy-duty cotton cloths for everything, first using them for washing up until they are looking less than savoury, then for general wiping and household cleaning duties, and finally throwing them into the compost heap. They cost pennies to buy, and by the time they've turned into beans and courgettes, I reckon they have actually paid me a few quid for using them. Teatowels aren't only used for drying dishes. I also use fine ones for straining, and keep a pile of old ones handy for general cleaning, polishing, and mopping up spills. They go straight into the washing machine after each such use, and are essentially free, while the premium kitchen paper sold for such jobs is horrendously expensive. If you've no fine (aka 'thin', or 'cheap') teatowels, have a muslin square at hand, and use this for straining jobs.

Coffee Filters & Grounds. If you use coffee filter papers, tip the grounds out and dry the papers, then stand them inside old tin cans or plastic flower pots and fill with compost to plant your peas, beans, and any other quick-sprouting veg. The filter papers can then be planted straight into the ground. Just like peat pots, only peat-free, and free. Dry coffee grounds in the oven, mix with a little bicarbonate of soda, and use for cleaning and polishing steel knives and tools. Wet coffee grounds can be added to the compost.

Cooked Food Waste. If cooked food really can't be turned into anything else (ie soup, fishcakes, rissoles), then the best way to get rid of it is to feed it to something other than people; whether this is hens, a fire, a wormery, or a garden digester. Putting food into the fire and then adding the ashes to compost means the nutrients are safely and hygienically returned to the soil. Wormeries and digesters are available from specialist green gardening firms. Wormeries are fun but need careful management, and digesters need to be buried deeply and according to specific rules. Failing all of the above, waste food can be flushed down the loo to save on dustbin horrors.

Cream. To keep cream for far longer than otherwise, add a little white sugar and heat gently in a saucepan. It will then keep for a long time. Left-over cream freezes well. Old sour cream is delicious added to soups and curries.

Eggs. Never put eggs in the fridge. To test whether an egg is old, put it into cold water. If it sits at the bottom it's fine, if it floats to the top it is old but useable in cooking, and if it floats halfway up the glass, it's bad. Cracked eggs can be salvaged by wrapping in tissue paper and boiling. Salt in the water when boiling eggs prevents shells cracking. To clean a flask or bottle, put an eggshell in it, cover with about 100ml each vinegar and water, put the lid on, and shake well. Leave to stand for some time, shake again, and wash as normal.

Fruit and Veg. Tired Lettuce. Wash ready to serve, then put it in a bowl with a little water and a piece of coal. Cover with a plate and in an hour or two it should be edible. Carrot Tops make an amusing project for children. Stand the tops in a saucer with a little water, or on kitchen paper as you would for cress. The top will sprout green ferns. Stand celery, chard, spinach, lettuces etc in cold water and they will last far longer than in the fridge.

Surplus Roots. New potatoes, citrus fruits and root crops can be stored for several months by layering them in a plastic box or tin filled with sand until it is full to the brim, closing tightly, and keeping somewhere cool.

Kettle. Save fuel by treating it regularly to prevent limescale. Boil half a kettle of water, add a tablespoonful of citric acid, then leave for around fifteen minutes to dissolve the scale. Empty and rinse thoroughly.

Leftover Meat. Can be curried, eaten cold, reheated in gravy, made into Shepherd's Pie, or **Rissoles**: ½lb (250g) cold meat, 4oz (100g) ham or bacon, a little thick leftover gravy or sauce, ½lb pastry, 1 egg, brown sauce to taste, breadcrumbs, salt and pepper, 1 tsp each chopped onion and parsley. *Method*: Chop or mince the meat and ham and add to them the parsley, onion, brown sauce, seasoning, and about five or six tablespoonfuls of sauce or gravy to moisten. Roll out the pastry very thinly and stamp it into rounds about three and a half inches (10cm) in diameter. Put a small heap of the meat mixture in the centre of each, brush round the edge with beaten egg, and fold one side over to form a halfcircle. Press the edges together. Brush each rissole with egg, then cover with crumbs or vermicelli broken up into small pieces. Have ready a pan of frying fat, and when a bluish smoke rises from it, put in the rissoles, two or three at a time, and fry until they are a nice golden-brown.

Oil and fat. Never pour oil or hot fat down the sink because it will block it. Various bottled or tinned foods come in olive or sunflower oil. This oil is infused with their delicious flavours, so save on the troublesome job of disposing of unwanted oil – and add extra gorgeousness to your cooking – by using this. Have a little pot beside the hob to collect up the fat which runs off from bacon, sausages, roasts etc, and use this for frying. Old deep-frying oil can be put in an empty bottle and slowly used up in frying off onions etc for making stews. If it's gone rancid and needs to be disposed of, drizzle it over cardboard or newspaper and use these for lighting fires.

Peelings. Peelings can be put straight into the compost, cooked up into mash for feeding to hens (see Chapter 5), or added to the stock pot and boiled to extract their goodness. By peelings I'm also thinking of cauliflower and broccoli stalks, discoloured cabbage leaves etc.

Plastic Food Bags. Junk mail and subscription publications come in conveniently-sized plastic envelopes. Slit these carefully across the top with scissors and they will make perfect bags for storing food. Magazine mailers are tough enough for the freezer; do though check that catalogue mailers have strongly sealed seams! Turn bags inside out and wash up for re-use.

Potatoes. Cut potatoes lengthways rather than across, and they will cook more quickly, so saving fuel. Old, unappetising potatoes can be peeled and de-eyed and used to make mash or gratin. Never eat green potatoes.

The Sink. Keep the waste pipe grease free, clear of blockages and smelling sweet with two tablespoonsful of washing soda dissolved in half a pint (250ml) boiling water. Pour down the plughole, leave for ten minutes or so, and then flush thoroughly with a kettleful of freshly boiled water. Repeat once a week or so. A strong solution of caustic soda will clear blockages. Pour down the hole, leave for no more than 30 minutes, and then flush through thoroughly with a full kettle of freshly boiled water. Wear gloves and treat any splashes with a generous dousing of vinegar. In cold weather pour a little salt down the plughole and this will prevent the wastepipe's trap from freezing.

Soap. Soap will last far longer if kept for a while before use. This applies particularly to good quality cold process soap, which is gorgeous to use, but expensive. This process can be speeded up if you unwrap new soap and put it into a hot oven, on a baking sheet or similar, until moist. Then remove it and put it somewhere airy and cool. In a few hours it will be noticeably harder than before, and will last a lot longer in use. Save fuel by doing this in an oven which has just been used for baking. Save scraps in a jar, then, when you have enough, cover with hot water, and leave to dissolve. They will create a jelly which can then be put into a pump dispenser and used as a liquid handwash.

Sour Milk. Use sour milk to make delicious, light cakes, pancakes or scones. Using sour milk also adds depth to the flavour of vegetable or chicken soups. **Curd Cheese.** Leave milk which is too sour for baking or soups longer, until it curdles, then strain through a sieve, rinsing over the drained curds with cold water, and then leaving to drain. The sieve can then be tapped onto a sheet of wet muslin, plastic or greaseproof paper laid on the table, allowing you to easily wrap the cheese up into a ball. Use this to either make a baked cheesecake, or add salt and chopped fresh herbs to make a savoury spread. If you haven't enough for a cheesecake (about half a pound/250g), freeze the little parcels for up to three months, allowing you time to 'accidentally' overlook another bottle or two at the back of the fridge.

Stale Bread and Cake. These can be revived by dipping them under the cold tap for a second, and then putting them into a hot oven for a few minutes. The crumb will soften beautifully, and any crust will become crisp. Eat immediately. Cakes and scones respond particularly well. Odd bits of bread, if still reasonably soft and fresh, can be whizzed in the processor to make crumbs, then collected in a container in the freezer. Stale cake makes a super trifle, and 'queen pudding' uses stale crumbs of either bread or cake. See Chapter 3 for these recipes. **Bread and Butter Pudding.** I save the remnants of loaves in the freezer, slicing them before I put them in. Once I have enough collected I spread them with butter while still frozen, make up a custard using one egg, half a pint of milk and a dash of vanilla extract, layer the bread with sultanas and brown sugar in a greased baking dish, pour mixture over, and bake for something like half an hour. This yields about six generous portions for something like 80p. **Mrs Beeton's Baked Bread Pudding** is made with 8oz (200g) dried-up stale bread, soaked in milk until it's soft and spongy, and then combined with 4oz (100g) raisins or currants, 2oz (50g) suet, 2oz dark brown sugar, I beaten egg, and a good sprinkle of nutmeg. Mix well to a dropping consistency, then bake gently in a greased dish for between half and one hour. The cooking time can be dictated by the temperature needed for whatever else you are cooking alongside it!

Tea & Teabags. Collect in a jug and use to mulch garden plants, or add to the compost. Cold teabags make good masks for tired, puffy eyes. Damp tea leaves sprinkled over a dark carpet, swept about with a clean broom and then vacuumed up will make a good quick refresher for both colour and scent.

VAT. Always remember that raw materials for cooking are not subject to UK VAT, whereas many readymade foods are. Every time you cook something from scratch you're not only saving the cost of factory wages, transport, packaging design and production, chilled storage, advertising budgets and a profit mark-up, you're also saving an automatic 20% in VAT (at the time of writing) on top of all these extra factors you would have had to pay for.

Vinegar from Pickles. Use the flavoured vinegar from empty pickle jars to flavour pasta sauces, soups and stews — and to soften tough meat, deliciously. Leave the meat to marinade in the vinegar for a few hours before slow-cooking, or add a tablespoonful to stews or pies.

Washing Up. Dishwashers heat their own water, so none is wasted either by going cold in the bowl, or in being run through pipes to get to the point of use. Running a dishwasher also consumes far less hot water than washing up, and if you stock up on dishwasher tablets whenever you spot a multibuy deal, these should cost you no more than about 10p each. Make sure you have Economy Seven set up for your electricity supply and run the dishwasher at night for maximum savings. Handwashing crocks is made most efficient by carefully staging the order you wash things. Start with glass and plastic, move to plates, cutlery and other slightly dirtier items, then do lightly soiled saucepans, and finish with pans and roasting tins. Very dirty items can be scraped with a scraper (the greasy scrapings then wiped on a piece of paper and used to light a fire) and then 'pre-washed' at the end of a bowl of dirty water before you change it. You should then manage to do the final wash on all roasters etc with a single bowl of hot, clean water — and minimal trouble with clinging grease.

7: HOW TO PUT UP A SHELF

Traditional fitted slat shelving might look impressive but it is really very simple – and cheap – to do. Get your timber from a builder's merchant rather than a DIY store. The price difference is disturbing.

Tools: Pencil, set square or carpenter's square, tape measure, hammer, good sharp carpenter's saw, cheap portable workbench or some other form of clamp, screwdriver, electric drill with 6mm wood bit, 8mm masonry bit, large nail, small spirit level, and countersink. (A countersink is a little conical cutter which gives a sloping edge to a screwhole.)

Materials: Planed strip softwood measuring 45 x 15mm (2 x ¾") or thereabouts in section. Decide how deep you want your shelf to be, based on the depth of the things you want to store on it. Each slat will occupy 3" (7cm), so the depth of the shelf divided by this amount will equal the number of slats. Multiply the length of the shelf by the

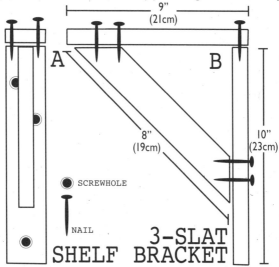

number of slats, and this will tell you the total length of wood needed. Brackets should be spaced no more than 25" (65cm) apart; a bracket to support a three-slat shelf will use 27" (69cm) wood, so multiply this by the number required, and add this to your total, Add 3" to that total for a four-slat shelf, or subtract 3" for a two-slat shelf. Avoid waste, by cutting the brackets from offcuts once the long pieces have all been sawn. You'll also need: a large pack of one-inch (25mm) oval wire nails, a small pack of 1½ inch (4cm) round wire nails, plus 3x 2½ inch (6cm) screws and 3x medium duty wallplugs per bracket.

Method: Cut the two square-ended pieces for each bracket. Drill and countersink the screwholes in the longer piece as shown in Diagram A. Clamp this upright, and nail the shorter to the top of the longer with two 1½ inch nails (B). Use your square to ensure that the two pieces are sitting exactly at right angles, then lay on top of a new piece of strip, and mark off the bracing piece. Saw accurately. Nailing this into place can be tricky, but if you drive the nails into the flat faces of the two outer pieces so that they are just poking through, then firmly press the angled bracing piece into position before driving the nails home, they should grip all the parts together and so avoid any slips or banged thumbs. Now it's time to actually put the shelf up on the wall. Hold the first bracket up to the wall at one end of where the shelf will be, use your spirit level to check that it's exactly upright, and then mark through the screw holes by tapping the large nail lightly with the hammer. Drill using the 8mm masonry bit, and then insert the wallplugs. Screw the bracket securely to the wall. Place the first slat on this bracket, and use the spirit level to position the slat exactly level. Mark the bottom edge of the slat onto the wall with your pencil, and put up the remaining brackets with their tops just touching the line. Once all the brackets are screwed to the wall, place the first slat on top of them, one inch out from the wall, and secure with two oval nails driven into each bracket at a slight angle to one another. Ensure that the last slat is attached exactly flush with the tips of all the brackets. Once you've finished fitting out your whole pantry, painting the shelves white is an elegant finishing touch.

RECIPE DIRECTORY

THE END